TURKEY HUNTING

BY KELLY ANNE WHITE

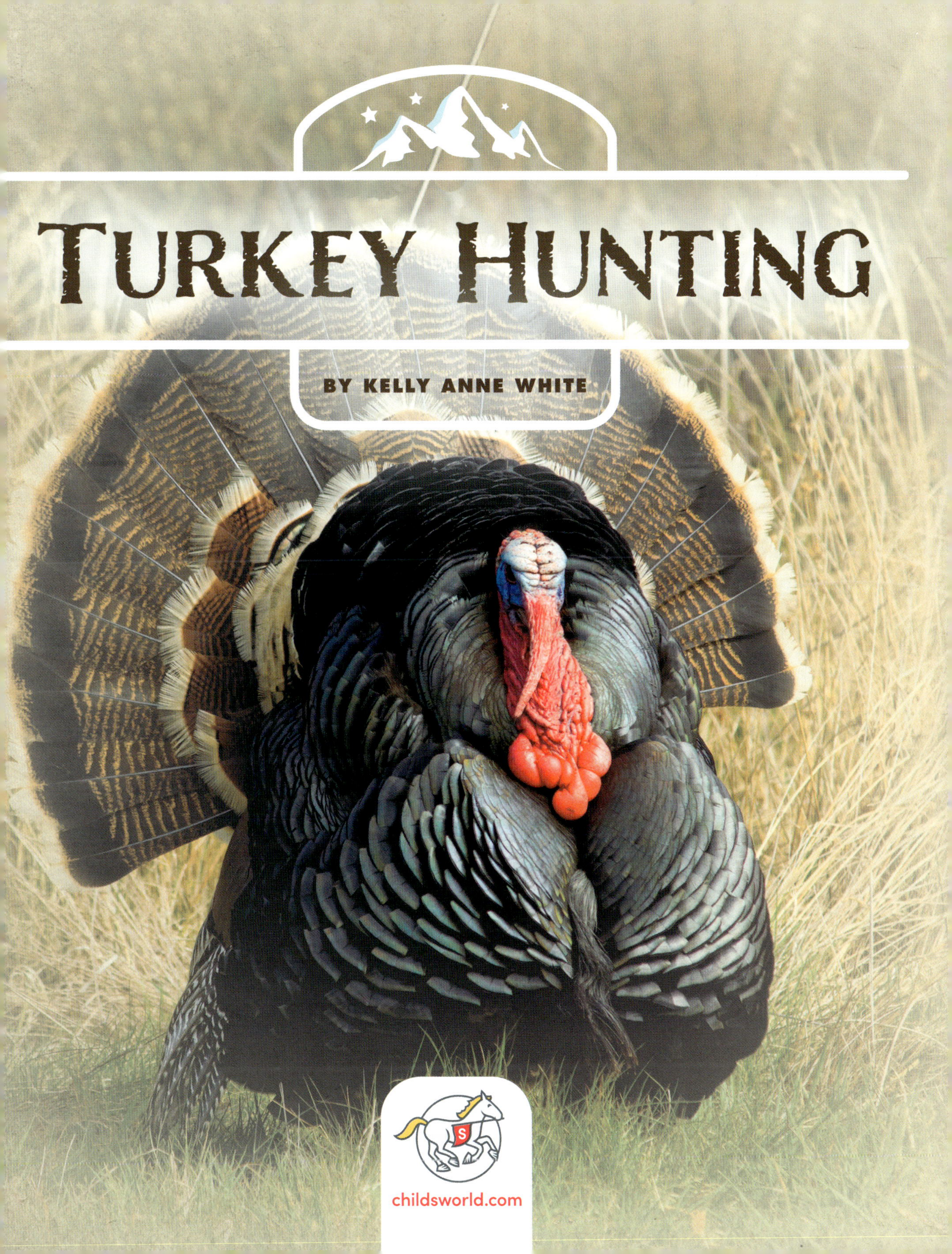

childsworld.com

Published by The Child's World®
800-599-READ • www.childsworld.com

Photography Credits
Photographs ©: Shutterstock Images, cover, 1, 5, 8, 11, 21; Bryan Eastham/Shutterstock Images, 6; Jim Cumming/Shutterstock Images, 9 (top left); Chase D'animulls/Shutterstock Images, 9 (top right); Sean R. Stubben/Shutterstock Images, 9 (middle left); Tom Reichner/Shutterstock Images, 9 (bottom left); Michael Chatt/Shutterstock Images, 9 (bottom right); Kerry Hargrove/iStockphoto, 12; Nathan Allred/Alamy, 13; Jeffrey B. Banke/Shutterstock Images, 15; Wavebreak Media/iStockphoto, 17; Treasure Photo/iStockphoto, 19; Jon Huelskamp/iStockphoto, 20

ISBN Information
9781503869769 (Reinforced Library Binding)
9781503881051 (Portable Document Format)
9781503882362 (Online Multi-user eBook)
9781503883673 (Electronic Publication)

LCCN 2022951243

Printed in the United States of America

ABOUT THE AUTHOR

Kelly Anne White has written many children's books. She lives primarily in Baltimore, Maryland, and she resides part-time on Chincoteague Bay in Virginia. Both areas are rich in fish and game culture.

CONTENTS

CHAPTER ONE

ON THE PROWL FOR FOWL

It is a crisp fall morning. Cindy and her dad crouch behind a thick tree trunk near the edge of the woods. Cindy is trained in bowhunting. She carries a bow and a **quiver** full of arrows. Today, Cindy and her dad are hunting for wild turkeys. Cindy scans the area. The night before, she and her dad spotted some turkeys roosting in nearby pines. When birds roost, they rest or sleep. In the state where Cindy lives, it is illegal to shoot turkeys out of their roosts. This is because flocks might get scared and abandon the area. But hunters can use roosting sites to locate turkeys and plan a hunt. They can shoot turkeys when the birds fly down from their roosts.

For now, Cindy stays quiet and hidden. Turkeys have excellent eyesight, so Cindy wears **camouflage** clothing to blend in with the forest. She waits patiently. She sees no movement other than leaves stirring in the breeze. But her patience is about to pay off.

Wild turkeys can be found near forests, fields, meadows, and water sources such as ponds.

Some turkey hunters sit at the base of a tree trunk. They stay low to the ground and wait for turkeys to come near.

Suddenly, Cindy and her dad hear clucking and warbling in the distance. A whole flock of turkeys comes wandering by.

Cindy's eyes widen at the sight of the majestic birds strutting past the trees. She sets her sights on a plump turkey that is within close **range**. Cindy raises her bow and carefully pulls back the bowstring. She makes sure the turkey is in her sight. She also makes sure no other animals or hunters are behind the turkey. By taking time to check her surroundings, she can avoid injuring herself or others. Once it's safe to shoot, Cindy releases the bowstring. Her arrow soars swiftly into the turkey's neck. The bird falls with a thud. Cindy has just shot her first wild turkey.

Like Cindy and her dad, many people enjoy turkey hunting. People have hunted turkeys throughout history. Native Americans hunted wild turkey in the eastern woods of what is now North America. They hunted with carved wooden bows and arrows. Tribes such as the Mohawk and Shawnee hunted turkey as a primary source of food. They used turkey feathers to make robes and blankets. They also used the feathers to **fletch** their hunting arrows. They even carved tools out of turkey bones. At that time, there were millions of turkeys in the wild.

In the 1600s, European settlers came to North America. They began hunting turkeys, too. Turkeys became more widely hunted and were sold at market. Settlers also cut and cleared forests to build homes, which harmed many wildlife **habitats**.

Hunters must be aware of their surroundings. Some hunters use tools like binoculars to spot turkeys from far away.

Because of this, turkeys almost went **extinct**. By the 1900s, the turkey population had dropped. Only about 30,000 turkeys were left.

State and federal agencies exist to help support wildlife and the environment. The agencies worked to help turkeys survive in the wild. They trapped turkeys in nets and moved them to areas where they could repopulate, or reproduce. Because of this, all US states except Alaska have turkey populations.

WILD TURKEYS IN NORTH AMERICA

Eastern

Location:
Eastern and Midwestern United States

Osceola

Location:
Florida

Gould's

Location:
Mexico, Arizona, and New Mexico

Merriam's

Location:
Western United States

Rio Grande

Location:
South-central and Western United States

There are five types of turkeys in North America. These species have a variety of physical features, habitats, and areas where they can live.

CHAPTER TWO

Hunting Gear and Methods

To have a successful hunt, turkey hunters need the proper hunting gear. Many turkey hunters use shotguns. Others prefer a bow. No matter what type of weapon a hunter uses, she should always know how to handle her weapon safely and responsibly. She should also practice aiming accurately.

Hunters should wear proper hunting clothes, too. Wearing camouflage jackets, hats, or pants helps hunters blend in with the environment so turkeys don't see them. Some states require hunters to wear bright orange, which makes it easier for hunters to see each other. Many hunters wear waterproof boots while hunting, too. This is because turkeys often live near water sources.

A hunter should always keep her gun pointed away from others.

Hunters often set up decoys that look like male or female turkeys. A male decoy might attract female turkeys to an area.

The ground in these areas is moist. Wearing the right clothing can help hunters stay warm and dry while on the hunt.

Hunters can also use tools to help attract turkeys. Some use decoys. These are fake turkeys made of materials such as wood or plastic. Hunters use them to lure turkeys to specific areas.

The turkeys are fooled into thinking the decoys are real birds. They may think the decoys are birds to mate with.

Other hunters use turkey calls, which are devices that help them make turkey sounds. These sounds attract turkeys to areas where hunters are waiting. Some turkey hunters can make turkey sounds with their own voices, too.

Many hunters use box calls or pot calls to make turkey sounds. They scrape a paddle against the edge of these devices.

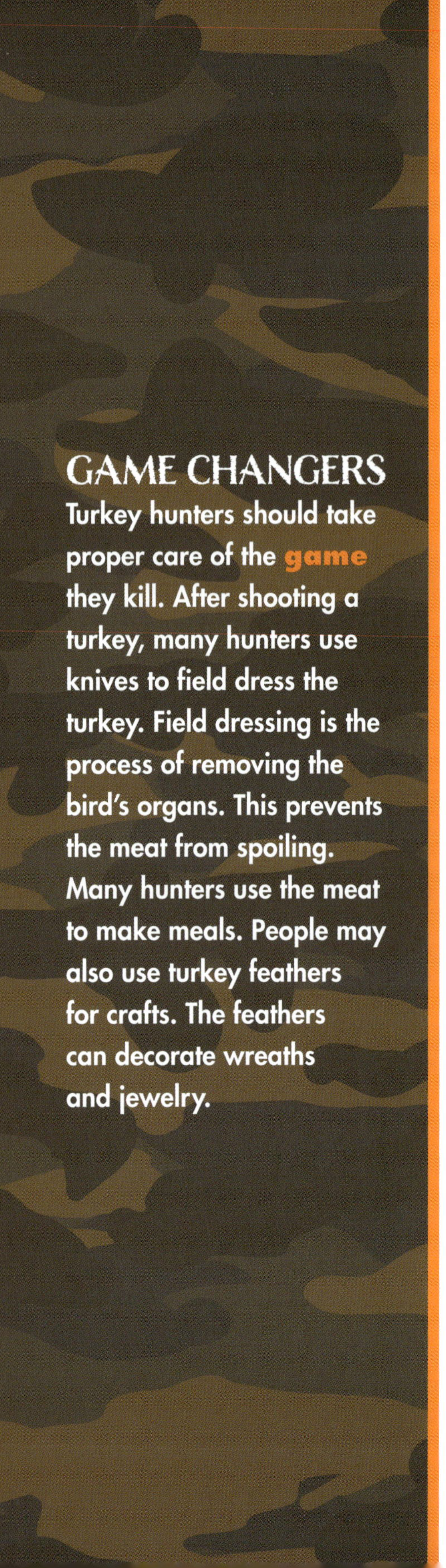

GAME CHANGERS

Turkey hunters should take proper care of the game they kill. After shooting a turkey, many hunters use knives to field dress the turkey. Field dressing is the process of removing the bird's organs. This prevents the meat from spoiling. Many hunters use the meat to make meals. People may also use turkey feathers for crafts. The feathers can decorate wreaths and jewelry.

Hunters have many methods for tracking and locating turkeys. They check the ground for turkey tracks and scratches. Turkey scratches are marks that turkeys make with their feet when searching for food. Hunters may also look for turkey droppings. The shape of the droppings can tell hunters whether a turkey is male or female. Male turkey droppings are shaped like the letter *J*. Female turkey droppings are shaped like corkscrews. Following these clues can help a hunter locate a turkey.

Hunters should also be able to identify turkeys. Female turkeys are called hens, while male turkeys are known as gobblers or toms. Males are larger and more colorful than hens. Young male turkeys are called jakes. Most hunters aim for gobblers.

Many turkey hunters like to get into position before sunrise. The best time of day to hunt is early morning, when turkeys wake up and search for food.

Hunters often set up decoys in front of their blinds. Then they hide inside the blind and wait for turkeys to come near.

Some hunters bring cushions or chairs to stay comfortable while waiting. Other hunters set up blinds, or portable pop-up shelters. They sit inside the blinds to stay hidden from turkeys.

Before going hunting, hunters should practice aiming and shooting a gun accurately. This way, they can make clean and **ethical** shots. Clean shots kill a turkey quickly so it suffers less. If a hunter only injures a turkey, the turkey might be left alive with a gunshot wound. Hunters usually aim for a turkey's head or neck.

CHAPTER THREE

SAFETY AND CONSERVATION

It's important for turkey hunters to make safe, responsible choices while hunting. A hunter should always follow his state's hunting rules. Most states require hunters to have a hunting license. This gives them permission to hunt. Hunters can purchase a license from a state agency or sporting goods store. Some states offer free licenses to hunters under 16 years old. These often require the junior hunter to take a hunting safety course. Hunting licenses help make sure hunters follow state requirements. The money from hunting licenses helps support turkey **conservation**, too.

Some states also have junior hunt days for youth. These are days during turkey hunting season when only kids are allowed to hunt. Adults cannot hunt on those days, but they must accompany the kids who are hunting. Many organizations even offer certificates for a beginner's first turkey hunt.

Beginners can practice using bows or firearms at a shooting range. They can also take hunter education classes to improve their skills.

THE NATIONAL WILD TURKEY FEDERATION

The National Wild Turkey Federation (NWTF) works to support the wild turkey population. It researches ways to protect the forests where wild turkeys live. It helps manage many woodland areas. It also focuses on keeping water sources clean and preventing wildfires. The NWTF promotes a code of conduct among turkey hunters, too. The code calls for turkey hunters to act responsibly by obeying all wildlife laws and safety rules. Hunters are encouraged to hunt only legal game and respect the land.

Most states have hunting seasons. Hunting season is the only time of year hunters are legally allowed to hunt certain animals. Turkey hunting season is usually in spring or fall. The seasons are set so hunters do not interfere with turkeys' breeding times, or the times of year when turkeys mate and raise babies. This keeps turkey populations stable and healthy. It is illegal to hunt outside of the hunting season. But hunters can **scout** for turkeys before hunting season begins. Some states allow turkey hunting in winter, too.

Hunters should make sure they have permission to use the land. Hunting is allowed only on certain land. Sometimes hunters can hunt on private land if they have permission from the landowners. Turkey hunting is also allowed on some government property, which is public land. State wildlife agencies and apps can provide information about when and where to go turkey hunting.

To stay safe, kids should always go hunting with an experienced adult.

To stay safe, a hunter should always tell her family members when she is going hunting. She should let them know her location and when she plans to return. It's also a good idea to carry a survival kit while hunting, in case the hunter gets lost. She should be prepared with extra water, food, matches, and first-aid supplies.

Hunters should be aware of other hunters in the area and keep a safe distance. They should make sure others can see them.

Hunters are required to report any turkeys they kill. They must keep the bird's feathers, head, and feet intact until it is reported.

Many hunters wear bright orange clothing such as vests, hats, or jackets while hunting. This makes them visible to other hunters and helps prevent accidental shootings.

By following the rules and respecting wildlife, hunters can help make turkey hunting safe and enjoyable for everyone. They can teach beginners how to hunt responsibly, too. This way, the tradition of turkey hunting will continue for generations to come.

Many states require turkey hunters to wear bright orange clothing. Hunters should also avoid wearing red, white, blue, or black, which are the colors of male turkeys.

GLOSSARY

camouflage (KAM-uh-flahzh) Camouflage is a pattern of colors meant to disguise or conceal. Turkey hunters often wear camouflage clothing to blend in with their surroundings.

conservation (kon-sur-VAY-shuhn) Conservation is the protection of wildlife and other natural resources. Some conservation groups protect wild turkey habitats.

ethical (ETH-ih-kuhl) Being ethical means a person is practicing good moral conduct. A clean shot at a turkey is ethical because the turkey does not suffer.

extinct (ek-STINGKT) If something is extinct, it no longer exists. Turkeys almost became extinct in the early 1900s.

fletch (FLECH) To fletch is to fit a feather to an arrow. Some Native American tribes used turkey feathers to fletch their arrows.

game (GAYM) Wild animals that are hunted for food or sport are called game. Wild turkeys are the largest game birds in North America.

habitats (HAB-i-tatz) Habitats are the homes and environments of wild animals. Wild turkeys live in several different habitats, from deserts to mountains.

quiver (KWIH-vuhr) A quiver is a case used for carrying arrows. Turkey hunters who hunt with bows carry a quiver.

range (RAYNJ) Range is the distance between a hunter's weapon and the intended target. Before shooting, hunters should make sure a turkey is within range.

scout (SKOWT) To scout is to search and explore an area for wild game. Many hunters scout for wild turkeys the night before a hunt.

FAST FACTS

- Wild turkeys were hunted by Native American tribes and early settlers.
- Turkey hunters have to follow many rules and regulations. Most states allow turkey hunting during specific times of the year.
- Some turkey hunters use shotguns, while others hunt with bows.
- Turkey hunters often wear camouflage to hide from turkeys. For safety reasons, some states also require hunters to wear bright orange.
- Some hunters use turkey calls and decoys to attract turkeys. They may also look for droppings, scratches, and tracks.
- Turkey hunters can help promote wildlife conservation efforts. They can respect wildlife, follow hunting rules, and make safe choices.

ONE STRIDE FURTHER

- If you were going turkey hunting, what gear would you bring along? Would you hunt with a shotgun or a bow? Would you use turkey calls or decoys? Why?
- Research your state's rules about turkey hunting. When is your local turkey hunting season? Why do you think hunting seasons are important? What would happen if people hunted outside of hunting season?
- How can hunters help support turkey conservation efforts? Why is it important for hunters to respect wildlife?

FIND OUT MORE

IN THE LIBRARY

MacCarald, Clara. *Bowhunting.* Parker, CO: The Child's World, 2024.

Potter, Jonathan. *We're Going Turkey Hunting.* New York, NY: PowerKids Press, 2017.

Uhl, Xina M., and Kate Canino. *Insider Tips for Hunting Turkey.* New York, NY: Rosen Central, 2018.

ON THE WEB

Visit our website for links about turkey hunting:
childsworld.com/links

Note to Parents, Caregivers, Teachers, and Librarians: We routinely verify our Web links to make sure they are safe and active sites. So encourage your readers to check them out!

INDEX